ISBN 1 85103 310 6

Originally published as *Ludwig van Beethoven Découverte des Musiciens* jointly by Editions Gallimard Jeunesse & Erato Disques.

© & ℗ 1998 by Editions Gallimard Jeunesse & Erato Disques.

This edition first published in the United Kingdom jointly by Moonlight Publishing Ltd, The King's Manor, East Hendred, Oxon OX12 8JY & The Associated Board of the Royal Schools of Music (Publishing) Limited, 24 Portland Place, London W1B 1LU.

English text © & ℗ 2001 by Moonlight Publishing Ltd & The Associated Board of the Royal Schools of Music.

Printed in Italy

Ludwig
van BEETHOVEN

FIRST DISCOVERY – MUSIC

Written by Yann Walcker
Illustrated by Charlotte Voake
Narrated by Michael Cantwell

It is 17th December 1770 and the attractive town of Bonn in Germany is lightly covered in snow, just like a picture. At the church of St Remy, Mr and Mrs van Beethoven are

HOW IT RINGS OUT!

Have you ever sung in church, at a baptism for example? Did you notice how your voice rings out? If you want to know why, try this little test. Sing first in your bedroom, then in the sitting-room and then in the garage. The larger the space, the stronger your voice seems to be.

1 7TH SYMPHONY, OP. 92, 3RD MOVEMENT, PRESTO
MASS IN C, OP. 86, GLORIA

in festive mood. Their little new-born Ludwig is to be baptised this morning.

Made to stand at the piano, Ludwig is trembling and crying. His father wants his seven-year-old son to be a genius like Mozart. He makes the boy work extremely hard: 'You must be prepared for your first concert in

NATURE THE MUSICIAN

Music is all around you. Nature is like an enormous orchestra in which the birds are the flutes; the streams, the harps; and the wind in the trees is like the bows on the violins. Why don't you try comparing the sounds around you with the sounds of instruments; it's great fun!

Cologne!' he scolds. As for affection, Ludwig can't rely on his poor mother who is always ill. In fact the best time of the day is when he goes for a walk along the banks of the Rhine. Nature consoles and calms him; the beauty of the countryside is like sweet music!

At school young Ludwig struggles with his lessons. When he is eleven he leaves school for good. For the rest of his life he finds even the simplest spellings and

NOW YOU PLAY!

Do you know that with only seven notes you can play countless tunes? The notes are sometimes called doh, ray, me, fah, soh, lah and te. If you learn them, you too could play an instrument, and why not get the whole family together for your first concert?

sums very difficult. But the child thinks about only one thing: music! He is lucky because he now has the best teachers for the piano, the organ, the violin and the viola.

Today Ludwig is celebrating his twelfth birthday. His friend Franz gives him a very special present: a big book of poetry and some of Bach's musical scores. Immediately Ludwig sits down at the keyboard. How

SING A POEM

If you like a particular poem, you could try setting it to music! Instead of just reading it, try singing it – let the words give you the lead.

Bach was already admired at this time.

wonderful! Every note seems to be whispering to him:
'You too must compose, Ludwig. Write something for us...'

The years go by... At seventeen Ludwig has become a brilliant musician. He makes a trip to visit Mozart in Vienna, taking with him his best compositions. Mozart is

FEELINGS

Music often expresses feelings such as sadness, anger or joy. In the music which follows, try to guess which emotions are being expressed.

5 9TH SYMPHONY, OP. 125, 4TH MOVEMENT, FINALE, PRESTO: ODE TO JOY

very impressed by his talent and showers Ludwig with compliments!

Ludwig is now nineteen and life is not easy. His mother has died and his father cannot earn enough to support the family. Ludwig plays viola in the Bonn court chapel

1 French Horn
2 Violin
3 Double Bass
4 Viola
5 Cello
6 Clarinet
7 Bassoon

6 SEPTET, OP. 20,
3RD MOVEMENT, TEMPO DI MENUETTO

and theatre, along with many fine musicians. Now he is earning his own living from playing and composing. He has great fun travelling and performing with his friends.

AMONG FRIENDS

Why don't you too form a little orchestra? Get together with your best friends and each choose a part: one can sing, another clap and the third can whistle. You'll find that even without instruments it can be fun!

At twenty-two Ludwig gets to know Haydn. The famous musician makes him his friend and offers him valuable advice about composition. For Ludwig his childhood is now over. From now on people will refer to him as the great Beethoven!

MUSIC IN HIS HEAD

A musician uses his ears above all; but Beethoven became deaf in his late twenties. In order to continue to play and compose, he depended on his memory; every note had to be in the right place. Listen to this music and, when it is finished, try to hear the tune in your head, without humming it. You will soon understand what determination and courage Beethoven needed.

7 8TH SYMPHONY, OP. 93, 1ST MOVEMENT, ALLEGRO VIVACE E CON BRIO

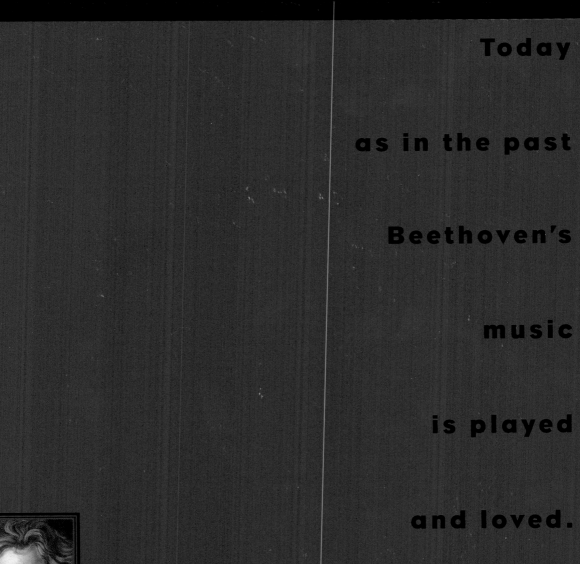

Today

as in the past

Beethoven's

music

is played

and loved.

THE 'MOONLIGHT' SONATA

From an early age Beethoven wrote music for his favourite instrument, the piano. His improvisations on the keyboard were always a great success. Every note resonated with feeling, and his audience was immediately captivated by the sound! In all Beethoven composed thirty-two sonatas, among them the 'Pathétique', the 'Appassionata' and, of course, the famous 'Moonlight' Sonata.

This piano belonged to Beethoven. A brilliant pianist, Beethoven continued to play until he became stone deaf.

Beethoven had so much music in his head and wrote it down so fast that his scores are often difficult to read.

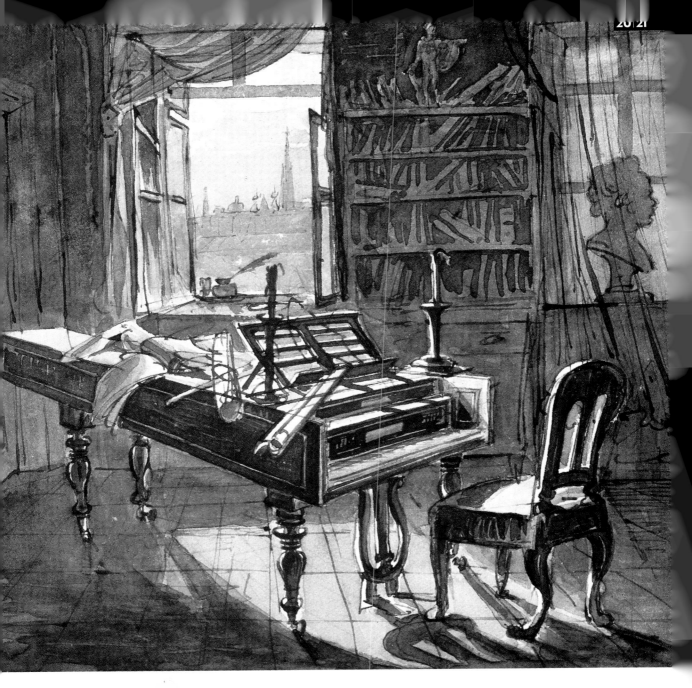

THE HORN SONATA

Beethoven also wrote music for small groups of instruments: two, three, four, five, sometimes more. This type of music is called chamber music. Here, too, he had immediate success: the finest salons in Vienna could not wait to invite the young musician to play for them. He became the talk of the town, and his audiences greatly appreciated, among others, his sonata for horn and piano.

Beethoven composed many, many pieces for string instruments, particularly for trios and quartets.

A sonata is a piece of music written for one or two solo instruments, usually in three or four sections, called movements. Many sonatas have been written for the piano, but a sonata for the horn is rarer.

9 HORN SONATA, OP. 17, 1ST MOVEMENT, ALLEGRO MODERATO

THE FIFTH SYMPHONY

By 1803 Beethoven had acquired great confidence and maturity in his compositions. He decided to write for large instrumental ensembles. When one instrument is in conversation with a whole orchestra, the work is called a concerto. For example, in the concerto you are about to hear, the piano is the principal instrument. When all the instruments are equally important, the piece is a symphony. Listen to this extract from the Fifth Symphony.

Beethoven often conducted his own symphonies.

In an orchestra all the musicians have their own positions. The strings are always the instruments nearest the conductor.

FIDELIO

Beethoven also loved writing music for the voice. He wrote several beautiful songs and arranged many folk melodies. The dramatic sound of voices accompanied by an orchestra thrilled him and so he wrote choral music like the *Missa solemnis* and an opera, *Fidelio*. When Beethoven died in 1827, he left us the wonderful gift of his rich and varied musical works.

An opera singer must be able to sing, of course, but he must also be able to act just like in the theatre.

The way an opera is presented depends on the director and the fashion of the day.

MOONLIGHT PUBLISHING

Translator:
Penelope Stanley-Baker

ABRSM (PUBLISHING) LTD

Project manager:
Leslie East

Assisted by:
Susie Gosling

Text editor:
Lilija Zobens

Editorial supervision:
Caroline Perkins & Rosie Welch

Production:
Simon Mathews

English narration recording:
Ken Blair of BMP Recording

ERATO DISQUES

Artistic and Production Director:
Ysabelle Van Wersch-Cot

LIST OF ILLUSTRATIONS

KEY: **t** = top   **m** = middle   **b** = bottom
       r = right   **l** = left

PHOTOGRAPHIC ACKNOWLEDGEMENTS

Archiv für Kunst und Geschichte, Paris **6**, **9**, **10**, **12**, **18**, **19**, **20t**, **21**, **27**. Bernand **26t**, **26b**. Colette Masson/Enguerand **26m**. Édimédia **23**. G. Dagli Orti **20m**, **22t**. Harlingue-Viollet **24t**. Holzbachova/Benet/Gallimard **15**. James Prunier **24b**. Jean-Loup Charmet **24m**. Ph. Coqueux/Specto **20b**, **22m**, **22b**, **25**. Pierre-Marie Valat **16**.

CD

1. A day to celebrate
7th Symphony, Op. 92,
3rd movement, Presto
Berlin Philharmonic
Conducted by Joseph Keilberth
4509 99637 2
℗ Teldec Classics International GmbH
1960

Mass in C, Op. 86,
Gloria
Orchestra and Choir of the
Gulbenkian Foundation
Conducted by Michel Corboz
0630 17930 2
℗ Erato Classics SNC, Paris,
France 1990

2. A very stern father
6th Symphony, Op. 68, 'Pastoral',
1st movement,
Allegro ma non troppo
New Philharmonia Orchestra
Conducted by Theodor Guschlbauer
4509 99637 2
℗ Erato Classics, SNC, Paris,
France 1974

3. At school
Sonatina in G major, Anh. 5,
Moderato
Georges Pludermacher, piano
0630 16244 2
℗ Erato Disques S.A., Paris,
France 1996

4. The perfect present
Piano Sonata No. 19, Op. 49
No. 1, Rondo
Jean-Bernard Pommier, piano
2292 45812 2
℗ Erato Disques S.A., Paris,
France 1992

5. With Mozart
9th Symphony, Op. 125,
4th movement, Finale, Presto:
Ode to Joy
Alexandra Marc, soprano
Iris Vermillon, mezzo-soprano
Siegfried Jerusalem, tenor
Falk Struckmann, baritone
Staatsopernchor
Staatskapelle Berlin
Conducted by Daniel Barenboim
4509 94353 2
℗ Erato Disques S.A., Paris,
France 1994

6. A little orchestra
Septet, Op. 20, 3rd movement,
Tempo di menuetto
Swiss Chamber Players
℗ Erato Classics SNC, Paris,
France 1990
Coproduction Erato/Cascavelle
CASCAVELLE

7. On course for fame!
8th Symphony, Op. 93,
1st movement,
Allegro vivace e con brio
NHK Symphony Orchestra
Conducted by Wolfgang Sawallisch
0630 10497 2
℗ Erato Classics SNC, Paris,
France 1984

8. Piano music
Sonata No. 14, Op. 27 No. 2,
'Moonlight',
1st movement, Adagio sostenuto
Jean-Bernard Pommier, piano
2292 45812 2
℗ Erato Disques S.A., Paris,
France 1992

9. Chamber music
Horn Sonata, Op. 17,
1st movement, Allegro moderato
David Pyatt, horn
Martin Jones, piano
3984 21632 2
℗ Erato Disques S.A., Paris,
France 1998

10. Symphonic music
Piano Concerto No. 3, Op. 37,
3rd movement, Rondo-allegro
Till Fellner, piano
The Academy of St Martin in
the Fields
Conducted by Sir Neville Marriner
4509 98539 2
℗ Erato Disques S.A., Paris,
France 1995

5th Symphony, Op. 67,
1st movement, Allegro con brio
NHK Symphony Orchestra
Conducted by Wolfgang Sawallisch
0630 14464 2
℗ RVC Corporation, Japan 1982

11. Opera and choral music
Fidelio,
Finale
'Wer ein holdes Weib errungen'
Charlotte Margiono
Boje Skovhus
László Polgár
Barbara Bonney
Deon van der Walt
Arnold Schoenberg Choir
Chamber Orchestra of Europe
Conducted by Nikolaus Harnoncourt
0630 13800 2
℗ Teldec Classics International GmbH
1995

FIRST DISCOVERY – MUSIC

JOHANN SEBASTIAN BACH
LUDWIG VAN BEETHOVEN
HECTOR BERLIOZ
FRYDERYK CHOPIN
CLAUDE DEBUSSY
GEORGE FRIDERIC HANDEL
WOLFGANG AMADEUS MOZART
HENRY PURCELL
FRANZ SCHUBERT
ANTONIO VIVALDI